This Notebook Belongs To:

____

43285789R00057

Made in the USA
Lexington, KY
27 June 2019